REMEMBERED

Adventures with Past Life Regression

Gavin Bowtell

Gavin Bowtell Books & Media

The information in this book should not be treated as a substitute for professional medical advice.
Any use of the information in this book is at the reader's discretion and risk.
Neither the author, nor the publisher, can be held responsible for any loss, claim or damage arising out of the use or misuse of the contents of this book.

Hardback ISBN 978-1-7393819-3-6
Cover design by Gavin Bowtell using Canva.
Publisher & Author Gavin Bowtell
Printed on demand

In Loving Memory of
Louisa Browne

FOREWORD

The contents of this work will appeal to both therapists and those who seek knowledge of their previous lifetimes; an invaluable handbook to give insight to this fascinating subject. We all have memories from our many previous lifetimes, hidden away in our minds and usually they cannot be reached. Past life regression is the key to unlocking the door to all these memories and experiences. When being regressed to a past life, the memories, feelings and emotions can all be experienced within the mind's eye; it's like a vivid daydream. Past life regression also has therapeutic benefits, and can help release trapped emotions and traumas which can affect an individual's present life. With thirty years of experience, I have regressed many thousands of people. To help promote this powerful technique I founded the Past Life Therapists Association in order to recognise, train and support therapists. I have now retired and handed the organisation over to the capable hands of Gavin, the author of this book, who has successfully taken it forward.

Andrew Hillsdon. July 2025.

PREFACE

The first time I observed a past life regression I was still in training. PLR was used to address an intractable smoking addiction. During the regression the client gave details of a past life as a WW2 pilot shot down somewhere over Nazi occupied Europe during a reconnaissance mission. The client recounted how an engine had caught fire, the descent and spin of the aircraft, where it crashed and that all but one of the crew of six died. He gave the date, make and model of plane and the name of the pilot.

After two weeks and some internet research one of my fellow students was able to verify to their satisfaction the veracity of the details revealed during the regression! No one believed this was fakery, but was it a case of cryptomnesia, or a genuinely recalled past life?
That was where my own interest in PLR began.

When I started writing this book I had two broad groupings of people in mind. One of those groups comprises those who are interested in past life regression, who might even be considering undergoing a past life regression simply for the experience or to resolve a problem. The other group I had in mind includes the hypnotherapists who may or may not have been taught past life regression, but for one reason or another have decided to investigate the matter in more detail. Whichever group you are in, or perhaps you straddle both, I hope that you enjoy this book and find something in it to fascinate and inspire you.

It could come as a surprise to the general reader to learn that not all hypnotherapists are taught past life regression. It's very important to understand that a therapist who hasn't been trained in past life regression can still be a very good hypnotherapist. There isn't a national curriculum for hypnotherapists - thank goodness - which means that a training school can put together a course which is based upon the interests and strengths of its teachers. This is a good thing, because it means that the trainee therapist will be taught by someone who is skilled and passionate about what they teach.

It just so happens I was taught past life regression and inter-life therapy (life between life) in my original training with the late David Owen, but I was more interested in other things at the time. I came to past life regression later.
Some training schools dismiss past life regression as a "New Age" distraction and assert that it has nothing to do with therapy. Naturally that is an opinion I do not share; the reasons for this should become clear as you read this book.

I would like to assure you, before we continue, that the cases mentioned in this book have been included with the consent of the persons concerned. None of the names are real. All the locations and personal details have been changed to preserve anonymity. Some case studies are portmanteaux of assorted facets of various cases allowing for the concepts and phenomena to be discussed without breach of privacy.
I would also like to add, before we launch into the main text, that you should not feel obliged to accept any of these past life regressions as factual. Whilst a great deal of information arising from past life regressions has been verified as having occurred in the past which doubtless add flavour and excitement to the study, from my perspective as a therapist the veracities of the revelations are beside the point – that the process brings about positive change and healing is very much to the point.

CONTENTS

Title Page
Copyright
Dedication
Foreword
Preface
Introduction: past life regression and therapy 1
Regression, repression and rewind 3
A repression of sorts 4
Let's rewind 5
Where memories reside 8
The importance of imagination 11
Some past lives 16
The Communards 18
Big in Japan 22
A short (pre-life) biography of a Deva 24
Experience is a blessing 27
Once upon a time in America, or a warning to the curious 29
Ilya of Seversk, a short (but true) story 32
A not-so wicked witch 43
Emma 47
Philip's brief lives 49

Who chooses PLR? 55
Why do people choose a past life regression? 56

Historical fixation 58
Recurring dreams 60
Family tree research 61
Alien abduction 62
Choosing a therapist 63

Ask about insurance 64
When hypnosis isn't recommended 66
Serious mental health conditions 67
Pregnancy 68
Healing crises 69
Past life reading 71
Surrogate regression 72
Training in past life regression 73
Other books by Gavin Bowtell 75
What is EFT? 76
What can it be used for? 77
How can EFT help you? 78
What you will learn from this book? 79
What is included? 80
Supervision, Training and Continuing Professional Development. 81
Specialist Scripts for Professional Hypnotherapists. 83

Meet the author 85

INTRODUCTION: PAST LIFE REGRESSION AND THERAPY

Past life regression is pointless. At best it is a scenic detour away from conventional therapy. At worst it encourages people with problems in the here and now, to go looking for solutions in the past. Well, that's what I *used* to think.

When I undertook my first training as a hypnotherapist I really wasn't interested in regression therapy of any kind, however I had enough respect for my trainer and my future diploma to attend to what he was saying so that I might answer any questions in the exams.

Throughout my career as a hypnotherapist offering past life regression, I have been asked over and over again for past life regression for marital problems, for money issues, phobias and weight loss. I have refused many times. Years ago, Anna Raeburn used to have regular call-in show on the radio. With sad frequency a woman would call in and tell Anna how she was being abused or controlled by a boyfriend or husband. Not infrequently was Anna heard to ask, "Do you have a sister, or a girlfriend? Pack a bag. Get out! Don't give him a second opportunity".

I was always surprised by, and admired, the conviction with which she gave this advice. On many occasions since becoming a hypnotherapist I have been contacted by women seeking assistance with past life regression, for marital problems. In each circumstance that I have in mind the husband, boyfriend or fiancé was a nasty piece of work; I'm sure you can imagine his kind. They wanted me to help them using past life regression to discover what reason there was for their bad relationships. Each felt it was something in her past, perhaps something she had done, or a contract she had entered into in a previous life that led her to being in her current situation. Now I'm not saying that any of these women were wrong to think that; for all I know they were quite correct. But to my mind it wasn't really to the point. Therefore, I was not surprised when I heard myself say, "I am very sorry to hear this, but the solution to your problem is very much of *this* life. I am not going to help you find the strength to tolerate the man you have been unfortunate enough to fall in love with, especially not when his behaviour is likely to have such a detrimental effect on your children. If you want to leave him, I will help you find the courage. If you want to provide for your children a healthier and more positive example of marriage and motherhood by leaving that a***hole, then I will help you. But I am not going to help you with therapy so that you can stay with him". Reflecting upon this now, it is entirely possible that had we booked a couple of sessions of past life therapy we might have been able cut the past ties that bound her in her present time, but first things first! This is an example of the type of ethical dilemma with which all past life hypnotherapists must be prepared to wrestle.

REGRESSION, REPRESSION AND REWIND

A regression of a kind

In the poem "Piano" by D. H. Lawrence the poet writes of an evening event listening to a woman sing. The effect of the song is that it takes him "back down the vista" of years till he sees "A child sitting under the piano" and playing with the feet of his singing mother. This poem essentially describes the triggering of a memory through the association of the singing woman with an earlier memory of his mother singing. In a sense there is an element of emotional regression here "my manhood is cast down...I weep like a child for the past". This 'taking back' is the action of regression, and the form of *regressive behaviour* arising out of the regression here is weeping "like a child". The cause is nostalgia or sentimentality. You can find the poem here. https://www.poetryfoundation.org/poems/44580/piano.

A REPRESSION OF SORTS

Sticking with the poetry theme for a moment there is a tragical-comical poem by W.H. Auden "The Ballad of Miss Gee". In the poem the eponymous and sexually repressed Anglican spinster Miss Gee lives her life with a 'back pedal brake' in force. We can understand this as unconscious baggage that is holding her back. An unconscious sexual desire is repressed here. The purpose of the repression is to protect Miss Gee from the conscious knowledge of her sexual desires which, if they were conscious, would be a source of guilt and shame, and if acted upon would attract a high degree of opprobrium. The outlet for this forbidden desire, insufficiently sublimated through her religiosity, is a deeply erotic dream about the local vicar – here the poet references the Freudian notion of dreams as wish-fulfilment. The eponymous lady eventually dies from a cancerous tumour arising from her perpetually 'buttoned up' state. "It's as if there has to be some outlet", remarks Dr Thomas. You can find the poem here https://thepoetryhour.com/poems/miss-gee/.

LET'S REWIND

Regression is often described as a return to a previous state, usually from an adult state to a childlike one, as illustrated in the D.H. Lawrence poem. A further example might be of an adult under certain pressures who resorts to sucking their thumb or crying for their mother. What we are looking at when we witness regressive behaviours can be a change in behaviour and in emotional maturity, insofar as the person experiences emotions and behaves in a way that is inconsistent with their physical age and actual mental and emotional maturity.
In my own consulting room, I have observed grown adults begin to speak in a kind of infantile babble, as if their tongues had thickened or their brain lost control over it. Very frequently I have seen men in their forties regress in front of me to an adolescent state changing both their posture, speech, perspective, thought process and vocabulary. Not to mention on occasion the manifestation of fascinating phenomena such as dermographia in which a slap from childhood, that left a mark then, was restored to the face of the client before me. In another example, I had before me a young adult who had been grabbed by the throat by a parent and slammed against the wall aged around nine. During the recall of this forgotten memory the mark of four fingers and a thumb appeared around the throat of the client. It is also interesting to note that certain physical and emotional symptoms suffered and medicated for many years evaporated that day, never to return.

Regression in hypnotherapy is slightly different. We are not seeking to *infantilise* the client, nor to bring about earlier forms of behaviour, but to help resolve something that happened in the past, so that the present and the future are, and will be, lived without that 'back pedal brake.'

Those who are old enough to remember video players will recall that if you had been interrupted during a film you could pause and rewind the film back to just before the part you missed and start to enjoy the film again. I could have used an analogy of watching a programme on one of the subscription channels where you can rewind the action, but the video analogy works much better because for those of you who are too young to remember a video recorder, *you have read my recollection of something you cannot recall experiencing.* When a memory is repressed a person cannot recall the experience. Repression is one of many defence mechanisms identified by Freud which protect the psyche. However, something that has been repressed is not necessarily paused, not necessarily inactive. Indeed, like a pressure cooker on the stove, the lid is very firmly on the contents, but the pressure continues to build inside. The "pressure" from a repressed feeling or memory can manifest itself in all sorts of different way, in fears, phobias, functional neurological disorders, and physical illness to name a few.

Regression therapy usually refers to "regression to cause" in which the cause or causes are assumed to have arisen within this lifetime. There is a difficulty with this understanding of "regression to cause" as a label because regression can produce a spontaneous past life regression. Put very simply if you have a client in hypnosis and ask their subconscious mind to take you to the time a problem arose for them, it will do so, whether that is the current life or a past life. This is why it is *crucial* that anyone using regression therapy should be trained to work with past lives too – should one come up.

Curiously enough this can happen the other way around too. I have had clients come to me for the purpose of exploring past lives only to find that their subconscious has taken them straight to a meeting with deceased parents where grief work needs to be carried out to effect healing in this life, or in others cases where parental influences over the adult child are still very powerful and inhibiting, and need to be resolved for the client so that they can move on with the current lifetime. As hypnotherapists we learn to trust the wisdom of the subconscious, most of the time.

Just as a current life regression can lead to a spontaneous past life regression, so a past life regression can march you right the way back into the present life to finish work *in the here and now*, before an excursion through the *there and then*.

WHERE MEMORIES RESIDE

Whilst it would be ideal to begin this section with a discussion of what memory is, I am afraid that the subject is too large and too complex to have justice done to it in so short a book as this is intended to be. However, let it suffice to say that what human memory *isn't* is a complete record of everything we have ever thought or experienced. Most scientists these days agree that memories are generated rather than stored

As a former train driver it was part of my experience that birds, most often pigeons, would occasionally be hit by a train. Sometimes they would hit the train with wings outstretched and would somehow leave a dusty impression of themselves upon the windscreen. And whilst what had happened was very clear to anyone who saw these spectral impressions of pigeons, they were not a complete record of what was happening at that time. Such is memory.

Similarly, if you visit an old building such as a church, you will very often find that the steps have been worn away into a concave smoothness. This points to the thousands of feet that must have trodden those stones over centuries, but in no way does it recall those people to whom those feet belonged, though it *is* in a sense a record of their passing. People experience so many things during their lifetimes, sometimes over and over again so that they are sculpted or warped in one way or another, that leaves an indelible trace in the body or the personality, so that you would imagine the agents of such change would be noticed. But just like those untold numbers of feet carving a groove in the step, people are sculpted and warped by thousands of unremembered events in their lifetime, like the long-ago melted icebergs that carved out valleys in our landscape. I suppose we could refer to some life events as "unremarked experiences" – sometimes the most familiar experiences are the most unremarked because we pay no attention to them. Tying shoes or opening doors for example.

If you think about something that you do remember, a birthday, your driving test, giving birth, sitting an exam, anything: you might very well believe that you can remember every part of it. But in fact, just a few moments conscious attention shows that this is not that case. This is what I mean. If I say the word 'school', what is the first memory that comes to mind?

For me it is the cold-warm sensation of sitting on a dusty varnished parquet floor in the 'great hall' singing songs from "Come and Praise", a BBC publication of the early 1980s. I can still feel the uncomfortable sensation of the dust from the floor on my hands. I can hear the eerie creaking of the wood of the stage as its boards expanded and contracted, and behind the sound of the piano played by Mrs Bridger is the sound of the dinner ladies preparing our meals, as the smell of yesterday's dinners mixed in with today's offerings and the smell of the child in front of me.

This sounds like a rather complete record doesn't it? The fact is I made it up. I can remember the hymn books that we used, but I didn't recall that is was called "Come and Praise", much less the name of its publisher – I had to look that up. I knew it by the cover. This 'memory' is a composite of several of my unremarked experiences in a particular school. But the fact of the matter is that a lot of that *will have been my experience*, indeed had I not had these experiences I could not have made that up, and the overall emotional tone of that composite memory would not feel right if what I had written was outside my experience. Therefore, what we can say is that this is a memory of what *a school was like, or could be like,* since my recollections are likely to be just one of several hundred similar recollections partly formed of impressions left by the school in the *particular clay* of my memory, and partly filtered through our experience since and emotional states then and now.

THE IMPORTANCE OF IMAGINATION

What I am about to write here is true not just for past life regression therapy but for hypnotherapy generally and almost every other therapy that you might experience.

Let us consider a few approaches:

If you requested BWRT® for a spider phobia, for example, you would need to be able to imagine how you would prefer to feel instead of feeling absolutely terrified.

If you chose hypnotherapy for weight loss, you would need to be able to imagine yourself making healthier food choices, being slimmer, exercising more.

If you are a therapist, think about symbolic removal, you might ask your client to create a representation of their unwanted feeling or pain. Or if you use

Swish - you would ask your client to imagine two very different images of themselves.

Let us consider something else. If you wanted to make romantic overtures in the form of some funny chat up lines, you'd probably imagine yourself delivering them, and the effect that they have. If you imagined a bad outcome, the likelihood is you would drop the idea of a particular kind of patter. Of if you want to try out a new hairstyle, you might imagine yourself the day after the cut trying to make it look as good as the stylist did to decide whether you could cope with it. You might imagine the compliments you would get. Unless you could imagine some pleasant outcome of the change, you might stick with the fringe, or the buzz cut. Do you see what I mean? *Imagination is a power.*

It is a natural power and potentially infinite resource that we tap into every single day, so frequently, so successfully and so automatically that we hardly know we are doing it unless our attention is drawn to it.

There are those people who struggle with certain aspects of hypnotherapy, whether it is imagining a safe place, or in seeing themselves slimmer, or more confident for example.

There can be multiple reasons for this, but I want to consider two of them. Very often some clients erroneously believe that their role is a passive one and that all they need to do is to sit back, close their eyes and the images plop down into their minds as if I am broadcasting images into them. Just think about that for a moment. You are sitting there in my therapy room with eyes closed, passively waiting for me to put thoughts into your mind... That is rather worrying, don't you think? Whilst you were reading that, you might have had a sense of that happening. Perhaps the scene took shape in your mind, and you might have seen in your mind's eye, or had a feel for that scenario. Whatever you were doing in your mind at that time - even if it was thinking about brushing the dog, or making a run to the supermarket - you were using your imagination.

Then there are those people who distrust their own imagination, just as many people distrust their own experience of the world. It is possible that you might be one of them, though you might be unsure about it. You can easily identify a person who distrusts their own imagination or their experience of the world; they use words and

phrases like "kind of", "maybe", "possibly", "I'm not sure". They will often seek clarification so that they give you the answer that they think you want, rather than answering in a way they suspect might be wrong, but which might actually be more useful.

A person like this who chooses past life regression might want or expect the images, ages, dates and scenes to drop into their minds as if the hypnotherapist is a projectionist. Often they feel that using their imagination is fraudulent, that they are making it up, that it is not real. If you recognise yourself in this description I really do sympathise with you. I've been there too.

What I really want to get across to you here, so that you or your clients can get the best from past life regression is that imagination is not fraudulent - it is REAL!

Imagination is a very real activity which has observable and measurable physiological effects. Imagination affects and changes our reality. But don't worry - I'm right about this. Let me demonstrate.

I wrote earlier about "the sound of the dinner ladies preparing our meals, as the smell of yesterday's dinners mixed in with today's offerings and the smell of the child in front of me." Every time I read that during the many proof-readings, my nose-wrinkled, and a slight wave of nausea washed over me, whilst an empty feeling dropped into my stomach and I wanted to turn my head from those smells that nauseated me on a daily basis. The recollection I described hadn't taken place for around 40 years at the time of writing. It was nothing but my imagination that brought back those physical feelings from the past!

Imagine a bag of salt and vinegar crisps. You open the bag, and that tangy fragrance hits your nose and your taste buds ping! Or think about being hungry for a bag of steaming fish and chips with aromatic salt and vinegar rising up, setting your taste buds bursting with the tang at the back of the tongue. OK, for you it might be prawn cocktail crisps, or something else. But chances are, even imagining doing this you experience the effects. Or imagine you're sitting in a close, stuffy, over-warm room which has a sickly-sweet smell whilst someone hacks and hawks phlegm into a sample jar. Now imagine they turn to look at you, holding out the sample jar saying, "Would you like a sip?"

OK. Stop! Just think about your face right now; the expression there. How about your breathing. Is it natural and normal? And your muscles, are they nice and relaxed as if you were sitting watching your favourite TV programme? I expect not!

I do apologise for that last one. I could have written about

yawning to
see how quickly you began to feel the urge to yawn. But then you might blame the book and put it aside, instead of reading on till you get to the juicy bit.

I think you are more inclined to believe me now when I say that imagination is also a power and a potentially infinite resource.

By using our imaginations well we solve problems; using it badly we create them.

Are you a parent? Have you ever "thought" about how you were going to answer your kid's questions on where babies come from, on menstruation, what happens after death, or explaining why you and their other parent are splitting up? Have you taken on a DIY project at home, thought about how much wall-paper you might need, how it would look in that room that doesn't get so much light, or the order in which you will clear the room, or work around larger pieces of furniture? Right then you were using your imagination. That wasn't fantasy, it wasn't fraudulent. It was real. You discovered potential pitfalls and short-cuts and might have even decided it's better to leave it to someone else. But you did that using your imagination.

Imagination is how we work out the best way of being ourselves. It is how we plot and plan our domestic doings like shopping for dinner or deciding upon more far-flung adventure holidays abroad. It is your imagination that gets you from A to B. Your imagination enables you to see yourself in the future, happy with the person you are dating, or breaking the news to your parents that you are getting married or divorced.

Being able or unable to imagine this or that is a way of testing your feelings, of testing reality, in a way imagination is the sense through which your experience of reality is refracted, mediated and affirmed.

Earlier I said that the effects of imagination are measurable. Well, they are. Not so many moments ago you were screwing up your face and thinking that I am gross. That was measurable!

There are many research papers that provide evidence of the measurable power of imagination. For example, in the **Journal**

of Sports Science & Medicine 2016 Sep; 15(3): 434-450 "Effects of Mental Imagery on Muscular Strength in Healthy and Patient Participants: A Systematic Review" Silmani *et al* concluded that joining mental imagery to physical training wrought better results for improving strength performance and that it was also valuable in improving recovery in patients with short-term muscle immobilisation.

If you use any kind of affirmations, you are harnessing the power of imagination. Émile Coué, the pharmacist and psychotherapist, through his discovery that optimistic self-suggestions such as "Every day, in every way, I'm getting better and better", enabled his patients to make much faster progress in recovery than expected.

Hopefully you can think of many more examples of how imagination has had real world applications for you, so that if you choose to experience a past life regression, you know that you can relax and let your mind work as it will. I think it is quite possible that imagination in or out of hypnosis is a way of engaging the conscious and subconscious mind. If past lives reside in the subconscious - as some believe they do - then your imagination will be the universal key to unlocking them.

SOME PAST LIVES

Isabel Smith

This was quite a different past life regression from many of the others that I had conducted because the client recalled a great deal of detail.

In 1829 Isabel Smith was born. Not much is known of her early life. But one mid-morning in May 1849 Isabel found herself in London for the first time, aged 20.

London 1849 was a full of activity of all kinds. Karl Marx had recently relocated there from Paris. Paintings by the Pre-Raphaelite Brotherhood had gone on public display for the first time and William Hamilton, an orphaned bricklayer from Ireland, fired a pistol at Queen Victoria.

In the early part of the regression Julie, seeing London through the eyes of Isabel, tells of a cobbled London street, the stalls of colourful flowers and how happy she feels. She has by this point already described herself as wearing black laced boots with a nice blue dress of heavy plain material. As yet no rings upon her fingers.

"I'm looking around happy. Everything seems new and a little overwhelming. There are so many people, colourful flowers and stalls."

We then moved on to the next remembered episode. Isabel is now 30 years old. She is married and has four children. Their father is called William. Isabel described her happiness. She did not have a family until she married William.

"I think it's a party. There's lots of people. There are children running around and playing. Some are mine, some are others. I have four children, two boys and two girls, Michael, Elsie, George

and Mary. That was the order they were born in."
Whilst the children share their father's dark hair and eyes, he also has a moustache. She describes him as a business man. Isabel sees herself with blue eyes and blond hair tied at the back, reflected in a window. She is also wearing a hat. She remarks, "They are OK in the sun". I then asked Isabel what class or quality of person she was. "Upper class" – like her husband in business.

Final episode

In the final part of Julie's past life regression, she told me about Isabel's imminent death from influenza, aged 52 in 1881. She told me that she was in bed with bare feet in a nicely decorated room. The curtains were drawn, so she couldn't tell what hour it was. There was a nurse present. Isabel knew this was the end. William had been in with the children to say goodbye. At this point she was a grandmother to Michael's children.

Remembering regression

Very often clients ask if they will remember later on what they recall during hypnosis. Some people remember very clearly, but others do not. This is why I record past life regressions at the clients' request. Also – all memories change gradually over time, so a recording provides a faithful reminder.
After the regression, out of hypnosis Julie commented how it was "weird, it felt like me, but I was watching myself. In the first part I felt like I was on an adventure, I was excited and happy, then there was contentment in finding love." Seeing the end of her life she said, "It was peaceful, I didn't feel like I was conscious."

THE COMMUNARDS

Derek was 52. He came to see me with an anxiety that he found hard to place. He was confident in most areas of his life. He took a great deal of care in learning new things and was fastidious in his habits. His wife described him as "neo-phobic" as fearing anything new, but it wasn't as general as that. Derek's job is to provide administrative support to an area manager and their deputies. He had done this job for about 25 years. He knew it inside out. It wasn't the work that was the cause of his stress, it was the change of management that occurred quite frequently. He found himself "retreating until I have seen the lie of the land and know which way the wind is blowing". This was interesting because it revealed a certain doubt and uncertainty. We talked about this at length and of course he hadn't a recollection of when this all started, but he did recall that when he was at school he'd behave in a similar way when a new teacher arrived. Not unreasonably I asked whether it might be a fear of authority, which is quite common. However, Derek demonstrated to my satisfaction that this was not the case, telling me how he'd react in a similar way if a new kid joined the class at school, or if his eldest sister had a new boyfriend. He remarked that it was almost as if he'd always been able to notice changes in dynamics - "a shift in the force" he said - a Star Wars reference.

I then asked Derek if he could tell me about the last time he had this anxiety. To my surprise he said it had occurred whilst watching the exit poll of the 2024 General Election in which the Labour party won the contest. He told me he wasn't at all upset by the win, indeed he is a card-carrying member. But he said he left his house hesitatingly and with trepidation, all the while scrutinising faces, tones of voice, groups of people trying to take the temperature as it were; to gauge the level of danger. I was startled by this and asked him to think a bit more about that. He said, "It's almost as if I lived through times like this in the past, when it got violent." This was the thing that made me decide we would work with past life regression. As he stepped through the door into the past life, his immediate reaction was, "It's dark and I'm outside". "That's good", I said, "how do you know?"

Derek's face turned towards his feet as he moved them saying, "I'm on a flag-stoned path. I'm wearing sandals and what seems to a kind of tunic of dark cloth reaching below the knees almost to the ankles."

"OK, so it's dark, and you are outside, take a moment to see if you can tell me more about yourself and where you are." He went on to describe his wide sleeves and a realised that he was leaving a church, under cover of darkness and that he was a monk. I suggested he move forward in time.

He walked the path for a bit, said it was cold, and that he crossed a river by a stone bridge "like a humpbacked bridge." He then reached an area that was brightly lit despite the time of day. "There's so much noise, shouting, moaning. The light is fire, the whole city seems to be on fire." Suddenly Derek moved as if to sit up straighter.

"It's Paris! Paris is burning! My God! They are being burned alive. This must stop!"

"Can you tell me your purpose here?" I asked.

"I am a spy. I'm dressed as a bloody monk, but I shouldn't be out here, there's too much risk. I'm confused." Derek described crouching low to avoid being seen but running, he could hear the sound of his sandals on the wet stone as it was now raining. He entered a building he described as a palace where there were men in their tunics with gold epaulets and with trousers that didn't match the tunics. "These are the bastards behind this!" said Derek.

"Can you tell me what you mean?" I asked.

"Look, these people are part of the problem, they are behind this, but also under threat... It's all got out of control... I tell them to open the doors, that there are men and women outside being burned alive, that we should bring them in… Save them…" Derek was a little agitated, so I suggest he move forward a little. "It's all gone", he said, "I don't want to be here now."

I instructed Derek to find the door behind him and to close it once he was back on the path and to return to the garden seat.

Outside Derek was quiet for a long time. Eventually he said he had a lot of thinking to do and said that he felt like he has been several people at once, that it was quite confusing because he was seeing different aspects of the crisis simultaneously. Out of hypnosis he wasn't willing to discuss it much.

Three weeks later he returned to my office. Derek said it all made sense to him now. He had spent a lot of time thinking about it the next two or three days after his regression and that it was as if his memory was coming back piece by piece. He searched the net looking for the uniforms and tried to draw a diagram of the layout of the city. He was convinced that what he was "remembering" was the Siege of Paris and the bombardment of the Communards. He had been a socialist sympathiser but this was rather a secret because as far as the espionage was concerned he was a double-agent. The confusion of images he reported was, he decided, from the fact that he had had some idea of what was going on elsewhere because he had been party to those plans. He had lost a lot of comrades. I asked Derek if he could think of any way that this might link up to his anxiety.

"Yes! I can! You see it is the change of regime. It had all gone so badly wrong for us Communards - I literally had my fingers burnt. It got out of hand very quickly, and what had been home to me fast become a dangerous place to be. When I was leaving the church the feeling I had as I found my way was the same feeling I used to have when there was a management shift".

"Used to feel?", I queried.

"Yes. You see I thought about this and I realised that I was quite right to have been afraid - according to the way I was back then. I was a spy, it made sense to question motives, distrust colleagues, and check out the lie of the land."

"So, matters have improved?"

"Yes. I still don't like it. It's aggro having to get used to a new person every few months and the deputies have their little cliques that I'm not involved in that occasionally ask me for the inside gossip. I don't have anything to do with it. I've been in this job years. The biggest issues that have got a bit spicy were about access to a photocopy machine and someone drinking someone else's milk. I'm above it all now. I've realised what I have is a sensitivity for reading people. I'm always going to be wary, I think, its who I am, but now I know where it comes from. The fear that was there, that's gone."

I can think of many current life events arising in childhood that could shape a personality like Derek's to have such a problem, but would a problem arising in one of those ways shift so dramatically like that? Had we conducted more past life regressions and found that Derek had a wariness of and ability to read people in other lives we might have named that a 'soul trait'.

BIG IN JAPAN

In this adventure, my time traveller opened his eyes into a rather marvellous scene. He described it as a Japanese village with wooden houses coloured red with some gold, and the street remarkably paved with what seemed to be wood, placed in long strips along the road. It was a beautiful village nestled amongst dense forest and surrounded by lush foliage. The air, cool and clean. He finds himself aged around 13 years.

The next scene is one of utter devastation. "There was a war. Men on horseback lay siege to the village. They have moustaches and their heads are shaved, save for a pony tail that is held in rings. They are ferocious and blood-thirsty, killing everyone in their way, men, women, or children with a kind if 'fanatic satisfaction'. They show no mercy to the elderly or to infants."

He describes it as being thousands of years ago. As the raiders carry out their attack, which seems to have no object but to kill, an elderly couple help him escape. Hours, maybe days, later the boy leaves his place of hiding and finds the village has been destroyed. Burned to the ground. Not a house has been left, and everyone gone, presumably slain, or taken into captivity, yet the village is empty of corpses. Though his village had been very beautiful there is now nothing here for him so he leaves.

After some time wandering, at times nearly starving, he comes to a hamlet. The people look like him, and almost sound like him, but for a few words in common they speak a different language. They are also poorer. He stays with these people. He is accepted into a family. He works on the land, and the priest teaches him to read and to write.

Next, we move on to a scene very late in life. At the end of his life, he is alone again, but for a beautiful young girl who is his granddaughter. She was deeply sad that he was leaving, and she had even been angry, but forgave him for being old and near death. He had lived a life of forgiveness, somehow finding the strength to forgive those who had destroyed his village and his people. When he was very old he had a head full of shiny pearl-white hair - which was said to be a sign of his grace. Our time traveller did not experience his death here, but opted to step outside of his body to observe it. He reported that his spirit rose up from the body like a brown cloud, which coalesced into triangles and zigzags which rose higher and higher into the sky stretching out becoming light and thin enough to join "all there is".

A SHORT (PRE-LIFE) BIOGRAPHY OF A DEVA

This was one of those regressions that looks as though it might be about to go wrong. Although what we have here was the result of a past life regression, it might be seen as more of an interlife revelation, except that this appears to be a regression to a point in time before "life" as we know it had evolved upon the Earth. Indeed, in this state the client was, and always had been, a spiritual form of existence, so that what we did might be properly termed a "pre-life regression", or a "life before life" regression.

My client, Paolo, was an accountant. He described himself as having chosen a boring job because it made more money than teaching which was his real love, and also as having no imagination. He remarked that he was deeply bored with his life, his marriage, his children and "for fuck's sake I just have to get away, its grinding me down." I thought it unlikely that he lacked imagination especially as he had been very religious in his earlier life. Most religions teach by parables, and about places we have never been – and to internalise the meanings of these things we must have imagination to some extent. Paolo had abandoned the religion he was born into, because he felt drawn to eastern religions forbidden to him, which seemed to me a point of some possible significance. There was also the fact that he felt he needed to get away, the sense – imagined? – that there was a better life waiting for him. Paolo went very quickly into hypnosis, and very quickly entered into a past life. I asked the usual questions, but for some considerable time, he was silent. I might have mistaken this for slumber, but for the fact his breathing had taken on an unnatural pattern – a long slow intake of air, followed by a swift and noisy exhalation. As if bellows were breathing for him that collapsed as soon as they reached maximum input. Eventually he spoke, slowly and deliberately along each in-breath. He began to tell me about a time when the gods moved like spheres in an orbit, their movement creating a sound outside the range of any animal's hearing, but of a frequency so powerful that it brought all matter into being, and that as the gods played and warred with each other, made peace, and meditated, trillions of universes came into being, children of the thoughts of the gods. He revealed that he was indeed a god, deva, or spirit of a prehistoric planet that had ceased to exist so long ago.

"I'm falling. Falling. Falling. I am falling so fast that I can't tell if it is I that moves, or the universe that moves howling past me." Some few minutes passed, after which he reported that he "felt disgusted by flesh at first", that it "smelled". I was baffled and asked what he meant. Lots more silence and then: "It is difficult for me to explain to you, I need to translate for you not only the words of my language, but need to clothe those words with thoughts familiar to your world, those are so far different from mine there are barely words. I was a great spirit; my life was meditation and peace. Sublime peace. Then one day I looked into the future and saw your world so different from my own, with lives so fragile and so brief they hardly counted at all. But I saw the mighty passion and strength that love gave to humans and I desired it. I desired a wife for myself and to know that power you call love. That caused my fall, and I fell for millennia until my first incarnation on your planet."

This monologue ended and I nearly fell off my chair. t was also interesting to note that whilst my client spoke with a European accent out of hypnosis, in hypnosis it was incredibly 'London' in character and tone. I was about to ask for more information when the client began to bring himself out of hypnosis, so I facilitated that and sat quietly whilst the client looked at his hands. I expected him to say something like, "Well that was weird", or ask the time or whether what he experienced was normal. Instead he declared that he knew exactly what it meant but that he was going to have to think about it.

He kept in touch by email for a few weeks just letting me know he hadn't forgotten that he had promised to let me know his thoughts – not that I would have kept him to that. Eventually I received a thank-you card and a letter explaining that he had been profoundly affected by the regression. That it had changed something. He told me how it saved and elevated his marriage, deepened his love for his children, inspired in him a re-conversion to his faith, and that he had gone part-time in his accounts work to be at home with the family more and to share his love of teaching with them in a way that apparently brought them much closer. I was not unimpressed by this. I cannot say by what mechanism, other than the PLR, that this all occurred. For several years, continuing to this day, I receive occasional updates on the path his "new life" is taking.

EXPERIENCE IS A BLESSING

This regression was rather short, but there were some themes that tied in with the life of the client. Immediately upon entering the door this client opened his eyes to see sunlight slanting through windows, with motes of dust dancing in the air. He recognised the library of a monastery. He is a Benedictine monk, and laughs because he is very fat which he recognises as a stereotype. What is interesting here, is that the client has almost instant access to the life story of the man he has become in this past life time, the memories of that man's life are present to him immediately. He has been orphaned young, and placed in the care of the monastery. He was taught how to sing as his service to God, and to use herbs to heal and flavour food. One of his roles was to provide relief to the poor living around the abbey grounds by taking to them excess produce of the monastery. Although the Benedictine brother had sufficient food of his own, he would often eat that set aside for the poor, so that there was not as much food for the poor as there could have been. Although he had been rescued by the monks by being taken in as an orphan, he said his insides ached for his mother and father, and that he ate to "cover" that pain. He also reported that at times he found it difficult to submit to the monastic way of life. He had had a harsh novice master, and found that stealing the food was a way of asserting some independence. In the last days of his life he became dependent upon others due to a stroke and could no longer speak. He could not say the words of confession aloud, but sang them in his heart. After receiving absolution just before his death, he lingered on for a while, until his soul suddenly lifted from his body in the form of a golden winged creature like a griffin or angel. It hovered briefly beneath the infirmary ceiling and then vanished.

ONCE UPON A TIME IN AMERICA, OR A WARNING TO THE CURIOUS

This was another brief past life, but it was disturbing and also moving. This client found himself in America in a place that he described as looking like it has come just out of a Western. He wasn't sure of dates, and couldn't give names.

Elliot came for a past life regression out of curiosity. During the consultation he was rubbing away at his neck which caused me to wonder if he would be comfortable enough during hypnosis, so I asked about it. He told me that he could remember having this pain or ache for as long as he could remember, indeed he had been taken to the optician aged six or so because the GP thought it could be eyestrain. There had never been a reason given for the pain. So I suggested we might think about using hypnosis with that in another session. Little did I know what was about to occur.

Elliot went easily into hypnosis, as he assured me he would, and opening his eyes into the past life he described being in a dusty room. I'll let him tell you about this in his own words.

"I'm a prisoner. Its early morning, still cool, but warming up. I can see the sun shining through the window, and I can see the dust in this room in the shaft of light entering from the right. There's a camp bed and a thin blanket, a piss-pot, and the walls are made of…hmm… it isn't brick or wood. I think…is it called plaster and lath? There are slats with plaster, but I can actually see through the wall".

I interjected here, "It doesn't seem like very much of a prison?"

"Well, that's because they know I'm not going to try to escape."

"Go on", I said.

"I'm an outcast now. A few nights ago, I killed a man. I was in a hot temper and a black man walked onto my property whilst I was quarrelling with my wife. I had had too much to drink. I took up my rifle and I shot him there and then. Even in the dark I could see his blood spreading out into the grass. I sobered up pretty quickly after that, and felt sick and ashamed of what I had done. The sheriff came and saw that it was a black man I had killed, and said 'You don't need to worry about this. If a – (I'm not repeating the word he used, said Elliot) comes prowling round your property in the dead of night, he only has rape, murder or thievery on his mind. You acted in self-defence. That'll be it. I'll see to it.'

But I couldn't allow that to happen, I couldn't just get away with it because I'm white. I took a life out of anger and *because I could.* That isn't right. I said I want the Sheriff to see to it that the due process of law is seen to be carried out. I didn't realise then, that this was a threat to all of them at the time. But if the law sought justice for black men, it would run out of white men to hang. And that is what they have decided to do with me."

Shortly I asked Elliot to move on to the next scene in this life time, which was the moment just before his death. He described walking the steps up to the scaffold and the stool that he was asked to climb onto. He told me that the noose had been placed around his neck, that the rope used was greasy, and that as the stool was kicked from under him he realised with sickening horror that they had left the rope too long, Instead of a smart drop breaking his neck, he was almost able to touch the scaffold floor with his toes that he was clawing at the rope, feeling his face swell, as he was suffocating. But that it was very slow, and in the end, someone came and folded their arms around his chest and yanked, but still his neck wouldn't break so whoever it was pulled on his body till he choked to death.

As you can imagine that was a very difficult lifetime for the client to talk about. The thought that he has been such a racist in a past life was horrifying, and it reminded me that not every past life reveals a heroic life, or one you want to talk about. Sometimes it is necessary to conduct more than one regression in order to put things into a proper perspective. It seemed to me that Elliot was never going to be the same again. He'd seen at first-hand man's inhumanity to man, and how casually atrocities could be covered up. He needed to talk a lot about this, to process what had been recalled. But he did get something out of it. His eyes were opened to racism in the world, and the fact that he could do something about it and was determined to "educate myself and become an anti-racist ally".

Strange to say, the pain in his neck had gone.

ILYA OF SEVERSK, A SHORT (BUT TRUE) STORY

This is past life regression led to me working more and more in this field of endeavour, and was originally going to be published as a short story.

It was an ordinary day when Matthew had hit a wall with what he had been working on and decided that a change of direction was needed. He stood at his desk, stretched, and yawned. As he walked to the window to let fresh air into the room that had become stuffy whilst he worked, Thomas jumped down from the desk scattering papers. As the drift settled, a brightly coloured advert for "Past life regression" was to the top of the pile.

Matthew was a middle-aged man, tall but still slim. He lived alone with Thomas – a black cat who came to visit one day, and then the next, and the next. His visits became longer, until neither of them realised that they had been living together for quite some while. Both took this arrangement for granted. Forasmuch as Matthew looked forward to waking and finding Thomas on his bed when he woke, or on the doorstep when he returned home from some outing, he regarded himself as independent of the cat, as Thomas acted independently of him. He'd been this way all his life, with everyone: with family and friends. Not aloof. Not even distant. Just slightly on the outside edge of being on the inside, if you see what I mean. Whether he was on the outside because he was an observer of those around him he had never known. The answer didn't trouble him all that much - thus it had ever been. But it had carried a stigma. Not from friends. No. His friends found him charming and hospitable most of the time. It was Matthew's family who looked at him askance; for they - loud, outgoing and boisterous - couldn't work out why he was so different. Many of them felt silently judged by his presence, whilst Matthew, not knowing this about them, in his turn felt that they viewed his solitary life and unusual interests as a sign of his inherent failure. "Hmm," thought Matthew, as he picked up the flyer, "Why did I keep this?" But he knew why. Matthew was a genealogist. He spent his days delving into the history of his clients, working his way backwards, adding details to the family history of the person that had come to him unable to go as far as they wished.

He had noticed on more than one occasion that there were unconscious threads woven through a family history: repeated tragedies, illnesses, and occupations. How many times had he sat listening to his clients telling him that they were the "first" in their family in some area of social, academic or professional achievement when in fact, the family tree revealed the truth? The truth being that they were really following in the footsteps of their ancestors. Sometimes even choosing to live far away from their living family, but now eerily close to that place where a great grandparent lived, worked and had his being. Time after time, what had long passed gave the impression of not being all that far from what was happening now, or just recently in the lives of his clients. Often, he wondered if there was some silent command calling out orders for the re-enactment of the same dreary dramas, generation after generation. And if he was feeling whimsical he wondered what might finally cut those strings being pulled from the past or appease the haunting ancestors. Matthew picked up the leaflet and carried it along the passage to the kitchen. He knew Thomas was following; he could hear the 'tick tick' of cat-claws along the floor. Thomas sat at the kitchen door watching the birds in the garden, occasionally chattering to them as if to charm them. Now halfway through a cup of tea and wondering what to do to clear his mind about the 'family' he was working on,

Matthew once again took up the leaflet and read about how Andrew Eastern, Hypnotherapist, could help 'discover past lives and resolve barriers to success in your current life'. "Current life!" Matthew said aloud, "I'm not sure I like the sound of that, do you Thomas?" Thomas, still watching the birds, cocked an ear. "It sounds like there could be more of this to come". Matthew was not a pessimist, but he was sensible enough to know that for many people one life was all that was required; another 'undiscovered country' didn't so much strike him as an adventure, but as an unnecessary labour best avoided. He was not given to meeting trouble halfway. Nevertheless, and almost in spite of himself, Matthew picked up his phone, and started to send an email to Andrew Eastern. As far as he was concerned a telephone call ran the risk of being answered there and then, and he'd find himself committing to something he wanted to do but simultaneously found preposterous. He was after all a rational and intelligent man, but he also liked to give himself time and space. Everyone said that, and that was important to him. People - his clients - came to him, because of the doggedly rigorous approach to history that he brought to his genealogy business. He didn't promise ancestors who were royalty, or rich celebrities of their time. He gave to his clients the facts. Hard facts sometimes; and where the facts permitted it, he would flesh out the timeline with a probable approximation of events, that to some of his clients, sounded exactly like the kind of story they had been waiting for. Andrew Eastern had replied before the end of 'office hours' and had offered Matthew an appointment that neatly coincided with his day off and was located not far from his usual supermarket where he could go shopping afterwards so that it wouldn't be an entirely wasted day. During that telephone call Thomas had leapt upon Matthew's lap as he listened to Andrew explain the process. After the telephone call, and not wishing to disturb Thomas who now looked fast asleep, Matthew decided to open a webpage on his phone and do his own research. As he breathed in and out so a tiny blue bubble between Thomas's lips gently expanded and contracted, looking dangerously as if it might turn into drool.

The following Tuesday morning, just before 10:30 Matthew parked his car. He double checked the address and finding it to his satisfaction turned his phone to silent before one last hopeless check of his messages and email for anything that might constitute a good excuse for not going through with what he had come here for. No excuse presented itself, so he got out of the car and walked along the street. On either side Victorian terraced houses lined a strip of tarmac edged with cars in as many states of repair as the houses they stood before. He arrived at 118. An arch of brick painted red was around the door, reached by a path that had once been very smartly laid in black and white diamond shaped tiles which were now more noticeable by their absence. Nottingham lace hung at the windows - incongruously Matthew wondered if that was 'normal' for a hypnotherapist's place of work. He rang the bell. After a very short delay the door was opened into a dark hallway, the walls of which were hung with bottle green flock wallpaper.

"Are you Matt, or Matthew? Hello! Come in. Welcome. Welcome. Mind the step. That's it. I'm Andrew of course, pleased you could make it. Go through; second on the right. Would you like tea? The kettle has just boiled."

Matthew stood uncertainly on the threshold of the second room on the right. "Let me take your coat", said Andrew "Make yourself comfortable - that chair over there. Was that 'No' to tea?"

Divested, tea declined, and seated, Matthew surreptitiously looked around the room. It was an intriguing room. It was mostly given over to books. One wall was virtually covered in crime paperbacks surmounted by a drawing of St Paul's Cathedral, whilst the others contained, aside from even more books, a wind-up clock, metronome, a photo of a black Labrador, and an amethyst geode. Matthew had been brought up to
believe that it was impolite to look at another person's possessions, and worse to pass comment upon them, even if complimentary. But he saw a book titled 'Healing the Family Tree',

pointed and blurted out, "What's that about?"

"Ah", said Andrew, "Dr Kenneth McAll - interesting man. Anglican. Medical man of some sort. He had this idea that illnesses can be caused by the interference of dead ancestors. He wasn't exactly an exorcist; more of a courier in that he delivered his clients out of the hands of dead dominating ancestors". He laughed at his own joke.

Matthew felt the hair on his neck stand on end, but just replied with a non-committal "Oh."

"Yes, it isn't to everyone's taste is it?" said Andrew, "Not exactly the sort of subject easily discussed over Sunday dinner without Pepto-Bismol to hand. But I can see why you would be interested in your line of work."

"So, he remembered that," thought Andrew, "or did he note it down?"

"I actually made a note of that", said Andrew as if reading the other's mind and smiling. "But before we get started, I wanted to get a few things straight. First of all, I'm not guaranteeing you will 'remember', (here Andrew bobbed his fingers in the air to make quotation marks) "anything; and anything you do 'remember'" - he repeated the mime - "Will not necessarily make sense now or ever. I want you to bear in mind that you are entirely responsible for your own thoughts and what you do with them and should anything unpleasant come up there is time after to go into that should you wish to. Everything said here is in the strictest confidence. Yes?"

Matthew nodded.

"OK. Use the footstool, take the weight of your feet, settle into the chair, and you might as well begin your journey into trance by allowing your eyes to close normally and naturally". The thought that "He's not wasting any time" crossed Matthew's mind as he settled himself into the chair, and finding already that he was somehow trying to catch up with what was being said by Andrew as if the sound of his words was coming at him, not only from a growing distance in space, but also through a passage of time that somehow slowed the words, so that they came one... at... a...

time... and clearly yet also indistinct, so that he found tha to try to listen to hear what was said whilst also struggli make sense of a variety of images that flashed across the inside his forehead like random images from a film: dew on grass, a red Cortina, candyfloss, a kitten, the itchiness of an old army blanket, the aroma of Golden Virginia, the cry of a seagull and then he was standing in front of a door. There was a number screwed to the door in cast iron numerals. He knew that, but Matthew couldn't make out what they were.

And he went in.

"Now close the door behind you", Andrew's voice came suddenly into the blackness "and just notice what you feel here if anything at all. There's nothing right or wrong about any of this...you can always turn around and leave by this door at any time..." The voice trailed away.

Matthew felt nothing. He was simply standing in total darkness. There was nothing there.

"Allow the environment to take shape around you whilst you look at your feet - what do you see there?" Andrew wasn't in this place, but his voice was there with Matthew, who looking down saw not the DMs he arrived in but clean boots, uniform trousers, belt, holster, gun. GUN! That was a shock. Then as he focussed on it, Matthew discovered a sense of true connection with the gun, as strong as with his mobile phone. He knew its weight, it was familiar, almost friendly, and its weight was a comfort as certain as the knowledge that he was exceedingly skilled in handling it and would readily use it to terminal effect. Then his shirt came into view and a tie, tucked into the shirt. At this point he felt a slight wave of anxiety - he wasn't properly dressed, his jacket hung upon the back of the chair. The chair was at one end of a table against a white wall. All the walls were white. Upon the table was an ashtray full of cigarette stubs. In his hand now, there was a cigarette with blue smoke curling up the tar stained fingers of a right hand. Another surprise. He was hairy. Much hairier than ived. Dark curly hair on his head, across his s and legs. Matthew heard himself describing ore he had really noticed it, in response to a to come to him, from a week ago in Andrew 's ger and shorter. How strange!

“Where are you?” asked Andrew. Matthew immediately described the guard room, and the sound. No. Was it a sound, or was it a vibration? It was hard to tell the difference. “I am a guard at a nuclear station. The guard room is very warm, and brightly lighted. I am glad of this. I am alone here. I feel content. There is a window in the door here and I can see that there is snow, very thick snow on the ground – all the way from the guard room, right the way across to the perimeter where the snow hangs upon the trees. The trees hide the fence. The fence is all the way around. It keeps us safe and secret. That is why I am here. It is a closed city.”

"Where is the station, what is the year?” asked Andrew from inside someone’s head - was it Matthew’s?

“It is in Russia. In Tomsk, actually”, he sounded incredulous at his own words, “and it is 1958. I’m a Russian.”
Andrew asked, “What is your name?”
It was as if Matthew’s jaw refused to open and his brain held on to the knowledge that he felt was there, pushing its way to the surface like a buoy momentarily hidden beneath the surface of a dark sea.
“Ilya!”
His name sprang to the surface. He felt a stillness in his mind and in his body as somehow this short, muscular, dark Russian inhabited that place where Matthew had been a long, long time ago. It was as if he fell into a deeper sleep. His joints felt lax.

“Move forward now, forward to a period in this lifetime that has significance to you. Tell me what you see,” said the voice.

For Ilya it was like waking from a strange dream in which he had been an Englishman living alone in a small house, too big for one person. He opened his eyes as he exhaled from the cigarette. He was standing in the middle of his living room. There was a sofa and an armchair. There was a wall unit upon which was placed a wooden bowl containing wooden pieces of fruit. Half a dozen glasses. A record player and five records in a rack. The records were placed at an angle to make it appear that the rack was full. A clock on the wall. The ceiling bulb was shaded with a plastic daisy now various shades of nicotine and tar. The walls had an oatmeal coloured wallpaper with a vertical geometric pattern in a shade of brown. The door to the rest of the apartment was behind him along with a small table against the wall upon which rested a radio, Ilya's favourite possession. In front and to the left of the wall unit was a door to the kitchenette. To his left stood a table with two chairs and upon it an expensive glass ashtray that others had admired. Of course, it was already full of the cigarettes of that day. It was early afternoon.

Walking to the window Ilya looked out and across the pathway below. It had been like a dream, what he experienced as he squinted at the end of his cigarette before lighting it. He knew that. But as he stood here looking out from the window of his fourth floor apartment toward the identical block just across the way - it had seemed so real. He drew deeply on the cigarette and blowing the smoke into the breeze looked down at the path beneath him and between the apartment blocks. The snow had long gone. It was a sunny warm day. The trees of the perimeter could be seen in the distance, but coming along the path here were two women. Too far down to hear what they were saying. He imagined they were talking about their husbands, exchanging confidences, or talking about their children, for they both pushed prams before them. One of the women wore a dress with flowers printed on it. The other wore a dress of bold geometric design that conformed itself to the shape of her pregnant belly.

Ilya was happy. He hadn't grown up here, but this was his home. He lived happily alone here. In exchange for the work he did, and despite the fence around the city he enjoyed more warmth and better food than others. He hadn't seen the others in a long, long time, but he knew it nonetheless. He had heard the talking. Yet somehow he knew he wouldn't be here much longer, although he wouldn't ever leave Tomsk.

He came away from the window, stubbed out his cigarette and reached for the packet to light another. He looked upwards to the apartment above, confused, and straining his ears, he thought he heard someone talking. "And just allowing that image to fade from your mind, move forward in time once more to the next moment of significance in this lifetime."

It was Andrey's voice from far, far away. He had almost forgotten him.
"Who is Andrey?" Ilya shook himself again. "You fool!" he told himself, "What are you thinking?"
As his eyes opened again he was in a hospital bed. A cigarette in his right hand – as ever. A small metal ashtray nearby. No butts in it yet. The hospital is painted white. White walls, with lights that cast a white light. The doctors and nurses all wear white - even white caps covering their hair. Ilya's surgery went OK, but there was nothing that could be done. And he knew it. This hospital is where he would die. But he was going to have a fairly ordinary death. There would be no pain. There was no pain now. He couldn't complain. His life had been of use. He had been taught well. He learned how to drink and tell jokes in the army. He'd been of use to his colleagues and neighbours, in his modest job keeping the city safe, he had been of service to the state. He had been his own constant companion. Well - he and his cigarettes. And now it is time to sleep again.

Andrey's voice again. "Just allow that image to fade, and when it has gone turn around and leave through the door. Good. Now make sure that door is firmly closed behind you and lock it. You can return here in the future should you wish to. Now...as you walk a little way back up that path, the sun is still bright and warm in the sky, though the day is drawing on. There is your garden bench. Just sit there now, and allow everything you have experienced, and everything that you have learned to consolidate...and when you are ready to move on, whether you have been able to make sense of that or not, just say 'OK.'"

For Matthew it seemed as though he'd been asleep for hours dreaming, whilst Thomas on his lap somehow contrived to make his legs ache.

He heard himself saying "OK" and then: "and the number is FIVE, everything returned to normal, and you are wide awake". Andrew's voice, close-to and loud. As Matthew's eyes opened, he realised he wasn't at home dreaming with Thomas in his lap, and the first thing that caught his eye was that book 'Healing the Family Tree'.

"So", said Andrew looking very excited, "that was quite a lifetime for a first time in hypnosis - you did extremely well. What's going through your mind?" Gradually the images in Matthew's mind settled and he replied, "I feel very calm. Anchored almost. It's hard to describe. People have always referred to me as 'a bit of a loner' as if it was something unhealthy but I feel connected to that fact, but without the negative judgement. Solitary but not lonely. Does that make sense?"

Arriving back home Matthew wasn't quite certain what route he had taken. He had completely forgotten to go to the supermarket. "Never mind", he thought, "I'll get an Indian". Thomas darted through the cat flap as Matthew filled the kettle. "Hello Kiska", he said, "You are not going to believe what I have to tell you."
Thomas looked at his empty bowl and meowed.

About a week later. Matthew was at his computer working on another family tree when an email pinged through.

"Dear Matthew,
In reply.
Thank you again for coming to see me and for the lovely review

you later left. I haven't met many people as hypnotically talented as you appear to be, for many people seem to struggle with past life regression the very first time. As you know, I leave it up to my clients to come to their own understanding of what past life regression is or does, and yet I read with increasing fascination how you felt compelled to look into the biography of Ilya. I have known this to happen once or twice in the past, but I myself was astonished to discover that Tomsk, or Seversk, was indeed a closed city. And how remarkable that you recalled the year of 1958 – the very same year that the Tomsk-7 reactor came online. I must admit a chill ran down my spine when I saw the photographs of the apartment blocks and the city which corroborate what you remembered exactly. But more than this, it is gratifying to note that the regression allowed you to re-connect to a part of yourself and find even greater contentment in life.

If you wish to revisit Ilya - or even search for another, you know where I am.

Kind regards

Andrew".

A NOT-SO WICKED WITCH

"I can't see anything. It's all dark. I feel like I want to go creeping through some woods. It's dusk and I'm on edge. I must be really quiet. There is someone following me, they have been behind me for quite some while. I cannot see who they are. In the distance there are some little huts. I can see them in a clearing in the trees. Washing lines hung outside. It's a close-knit community, but not many people."

Margery, our time traveller, finds herself back in the 1600s. It is springtime and she is an English-speaking young woman. She tells me that she can see the children playing, whilst women wearing white bonnets and raggedy dresses with white aprons over them, busy themselves with laundry and cooking. I asked her to tell me a bit about herself.
"I feel like I am a bit wayward. I shouldn't be out in the forest on my own doing things. I feel like I need to find my place here. I should fit in, but I don't. It's like they can't see me."

I ask Margery to travel forward in time to an important event.
"I cannot see anything. It's dark here. I feel trapped somewhere. I can hear water dripping and I can hear people moving around on the floor above. The floor is really cold and I am bare-footed here. I have my hands out trying to find my way to a wall. I am at the wall. When I knock against it, it feels very hard. I've found the door. There a really big iron handle. It is quite stiff and heavy. I don't feel like I should be able to open it, but I can. Now I am out in the corridor. It is very small and uneven. There is a light at the end, set

into the wall. Candles maybe, no! A torch!
I feel so scared. I've got to be so quiet." These last words were whispered urgently.

I said to Margery, "Now that you have the torch is it possible that you can explore this place?"
"I'm going up the stairs. There is a big open room, not much furniture, but there are several doors off it."
"Is there a window?" I ask. "Is it possible that you might look out and know where you are?"
"There is one big window at the end, but all I can see is land. Just rolling hills and villages."
"Do you want to escape?" I asked.
"No", said Margery. "I feel it would be very dangerous if I was outside. The people out there are dangerous. You see I can do things that scare them. I know things. I can feel a strong power inside of me. But I like to use it to do *good* things. The other day in the forest I saw a deer, and she was injured. I sat by the deer and I made her better. I can tell people things and create things, but sometimes they aren't very logical things".
I decided to discover whether there were any others like our Margery.
"There is just one other. We know of each other, but we don't know each other. We haven't spoken, but there is a knowing between us. We communicate with our eyes."

"OK, Margery. Can you tell me a bit more about this place, and how you came to be here?"
"I have the feeling it is a castle. There have been a lot of people here recently for a meeting of some sort. These aren't the sort of people I would meet. They were important people. I was brought here against my will. I was caught in the woods."
Here she sobs and says, "I shouldn't have let them see me. I should have kept quiet and not revealed to them parts of myself".
Another sob. "I'm so scared. I'm too scared to do anything. I feel like I'm going to die". Then came a terrible gasp, as Margery

brought her hands up to her chest, "They are going to burn me!"
Sometime later. "I can hear the crackling of the fire, and there is the other girl watching in the distance. I'm so scared and cross with myself. I should have stayed hidden".
Margery steps outside, led towards the fire. "I'm just a girl from a village and they're burning me!"
The utter disbelief is conveyed across the therapy room to me. I asked Margery if she would like to experience her death here, or to observe it. I also gave the opportunity for her to leave this place. But she chose to stay and observe, so I asked her to step out of Margery's body so that she could observe in calm safety. Margery stayed very quiet for quite some time. The silence was punctuated with small sighs and sobs. Eventually Margery spoke, "Just before sunrise she died. I feel so sad for her." There were tears here. "But I feel relief at the same time. I saw her soul float up there above the trees. She was completely on her own. No one came for her."

Our time traveller felt strongly that she needed to do something. She decided to help Margery's soul to pass into the light, by visualising this happening. She held Margery by the hands and said, "It's OK. You don't have to worry any more. You can go into the light". After a while I was told that it had happened and that Margery has gone into the light, but that there was a real air of evil in the place.
She made the sign of the Reiki distance symbol, over the area of the burning and then said to me, "I feel I need to stand here in silence for a bit, honouring her". And then, "OK. It feels much nicer here now. I am going to walk back through the woods now, and through the villages." At the edge of the woods, she said "Just one last look. That was really tough. I feel like that was a really tough life."
I then asked her to find the door behind her that she used to enter into this past life, to step out into the sunshine, onto the path, with the high wall and all the doors in it representing past lives. Once the door was firmly closed, I asked her to disconnect from that past life. She chose to use the Reiki Raku symbol which is

shaped like a thunder bolt and used for grounding. She sat for a while on the bench outside the door, making sense of what she had experienced. She said that it made a lot of sense to her. She has started on the path of healing with Reiki but was really uncomfortable revealing herself to others as a Reiki practitioner and said that she also felt welcomed and safe in the wood. She said that she really felt trapped in that life and related it to holding herself back in this life. I suggested that as she loved "the cards" she might like to do a reading later to see if that helped her to make sense of the past life and what it means for her now and in the future.

As she brought her cards with her she fetched them out of her bag there and then. She explained the card spread. First card. This is what you need to understand about the past. Second card. This is how the past related to the present. Third card. This is where you are taking yourself in the future. Fourth card. These are the resources you will need. Fifth card. This is the obstacle you will face. Sixth card.

She let out a laugh as each card was turned over. First. The message was 'trust in the unknown'. Second. 'Devoted and committed'. Third. 'Shed old skin'.

Fourth. 'Take care of your needs'. Fifth. 'Dream and Journey'. Sixth. 'See your seeds grow'.

"Well", she said, "Clearly I need to decide what I am going to do and stick with it, and continue with the therapy to release traumas. That what shedding skin is about. Taking care of my needs, is what I'm learning. But it looks like I must stop dreaming and start the journey and then I will see my seeds grow". So far as she was concerned, the past life mirrored aspects of her current lifetime, and the reading she made for herself tied together the themes that led to the conclusion that she must continue to work on herself, being true, following her heart and being a fully autonomous person, not held back by experiences of the past, or negative programming.

EMMA

Emma came to visit me to experience a past life regression. She was curious to know what it was all about and whether she would 'remember' anything. Her regression lasted around 45 minutes, during which she conversed with me as clearly as she would in normal waking consciousness.

Emma was amazed by what she discovered about herself and how much the past life regression helped her to make sense of things that had plagued her for all of her adult life.

In her past life Emma was a pretty, petite, passionate woman using logic and social resistance. She met obstacles and faced them head on. She was an American civil rights activist, fighting particularly for the rights of women – of all colours.

On this particular day she was standing out in the open, in a park it seemed, on a raised mound in the grass, delivering a rousing speech to women about their common cause, and answering questions with an impressive use of logic and insight, opening the eyes and minds of the women around her. There was a jubilant and excited atmosphere.

But then suddenly things changed. The police arrived, mounted on horseback and wearing helmets that covered their faces. They were charging at the crowd and women were being barged, trampled and kicked by horses and men alike. Suddenly a shot rang out and Emma wondered who had been shot when a pain like a punch drove through her side. Moments later she crumpled to the ground. The women tried to save her, but she was already dead.

This tragic end seemed to Emma to explain why she had been afraid to be strong and feminine in a very male dominated environment.

PHILIP'S BRIEF LIVES

In this particular past life regression the client had three past lives that really seemed to illuminate his current life.

This client came with an inability to move forward in his life, and with a belief that there might have been a contract in place that prevent any forward movement. I had worked with this client before and knew him to have mixed experiences with hypnosis, sometimes finding he was observing a past life rather than re-experiencing one. When asked to describe his problem he talked about there being something intangible that stopped him from moving forward. It seemed very odd to the client that he had been able to move on with his life when he was, by his own report "tenacious and like a dog with a bone", and as one who "never lets up, never let's go and is very much a 'take charge' kind of person". This client worked as an advocate in housing issues. The client entered his first past life through a rather plain, unpainted pine door. To his surprise he was a woman in this past-life and she found herself sitting on a kind of bollard or mooring post at the edge of the sea looking out to where fishing boats would return. She was enjoying the breeze upon her face. Although young, in her early twenties, we have no idea of when or where this life took place. But she had brought herself to the sea to be alone. Her father, a fisherman, had lost his life in a fishing accident on the sea when she was just a little girl, but his body had never been recovered. Since his death she has been trapped at home caring for her mother who was a most difficult figure. In fact, her mother who was ill and relied upon her daughter for all kinds of help, also blamed her daughter for everything that was wrong in her life.

It seemed that the only way in which this girl could maintain her peace of mind was to think only of one thing at a time, to clear her mind of everything else. Moving on to a different scene in the woman's life she entered one in which her mother was once again being very dramatic about something that had gone wrong, a small thing, that was being blown out of all proportion. She could not say what this was, only that it was such a frequent occurrence that she had almost become numb to it. In the scene she had walked away from her mother wishing she were dead, knowing that without her she would be able to do more in her life, but feeling guilty. She wanted to get away. I asked if she might be able to move forward in time to see if she ever got away. Moving forward in time she came to a lonely period of deep depression, a time when she was sitting again by the bollard, but by now she was older and couldn't remember her father anymore, and she knew that once she had had a dream but had forgotten what that was. She gave her age as 47. Her mother was now dead. She herself looked very ill indeed and felt that her end was very close. She felt bitter about her life; so much waste, so much unfairness. The client didn't want to see her death, but moved forward into the interlife period from where she was able to see her entire life. Here she began, very slowly, to understand that all through her life she had been responsible, like a parent to her mother. She had in fact tried to parent her. She came to see that this was completely impossible, and although she believed that she had in fact chosen to be born into that life, she couldn't remember why. She felt that it might've been something to do with the way in which she lived. She had refused to be a victim, as her mother had been, she refused to blame anyone else for her life, she took responsibility. But she could see that she was crushed under that. Refusing to be a victim, she also refused to let anyone into her life who might help her. She described this interlife period as having a stage that was rather like a time of healing. When she first died she had to learn to let go of being in charge, let go of being in control, before she could become fully alive in the interlife period.

In the client's next life, further back, Philip opened his eyes to find himself a man again, this time wearing a brown suit of good quality fabric and study shoes. He was in his 20s again, and in a wheelchair. His legs didn't work so well, and his chest was weak and had at that time an infection. He said he thought that he had been born perfectly healthy but had been stricken with polio aged around ten. At the end of the regression the client reflected upon the door that he entered through being a flimsy hollow door, and that perhaps the perceived weakness in the door reflected the power the past lives had previously had in his current life. Again, there was no date here, but he had a job involving shipping. He felt it was insuring cargoes against loss. Could this role in life be related to the loss of his father at sea in the previous life? It was a job that required precision with numbers and dates. Moving forward in life, his chest became increasingly weak. Breathing was so hard.

"I have to hold on tight, just to sit upright in this chair, I feel like all my life I have been hanging on".

I asked him what kind of person he had been in this life, what had his personality been like. He answered that "I've been held back all my life because of my illness, but I never gave up. There have been so many arguments. I am treated like a cretin because of this chair and I am forever having to defend my integrity against the imputations of others".

I asked him what he meant by that, and he replied, "I have, since being confined to this chair, been held as of lesser value compared to other men. Thus, I am alone and without a wife. Thus, I have no children of my own."

I was rather taken aback by the formality of his speech since the client did not speak in this way. I observed, "You are very formal in your speech, aren't you?" To which he replied, "And why not? I must afford myself the dignity that is mine as a man, even if others do not. I must show them, I do not wish to be rancorous and aloof, but they only want to know me as a benign cripple - not as I am".

I asked him to move forward to the next significant stage in his life. There is some difficulty here, so I deepened the hypnosis a little and gave the suggestion that he could just let the images form around him and start as usual by looking toward his feet to tell me what he could see. I was rather surprised then when he replied, "I am on the ceiling. I have my back to the ceiling. I have already died. I died alone there. I think it was my heart. I feel an ache there as if I had been running hard. I am floating above my body and can see the whole room."

I thought this would be a good chance to ask him how death felt.

"How do you feel?" I asked.

"Erm, I'm not sure actually. I'm a bit surprised to be here like this. I thought I was going to go on forever. I suppose I feel free."

I then asked "Are you attached in any way to your body?"

"No, I'm not."

"Can you leave that room?" I asked.

"No", he answered, "I can't believe it. I am as confined here dead as I was when alive". He swore and said he wanted to move on. So, we did.

"OK, so just allowing this scene to fade for now, allow a new scene to begin to take shape around you" is what I was saying, when suddenly the client started to cough, as if choking, and then to sob. Great body wracking sobs and tears streaming down his face.

"Where are you?" I asked. What followed was a very dramatic and profound piece of dialogue, in which the client's impressions were very immediate, and in which the client was very associated in the recall.

"I am in Palestine. Jerusalem."
"What are you doing there, why are you crying?"
"They are going to kill him. He has just fallen into the dust."
At this point a chill ran down my spine, and it was as if the ground lurched beneath me.
"Who are they going to kill?" I asked.
"How can you not know? That is Jesus, the carpenter's son. He was a good man, but they are going to kill him".
"Who are you in this life?" I asked, as the tears streamed down his face and he coughed more. Instead of answering that he said, "It's so hard to see; the people are so much taller than me. I am only a boy, their legs are in the way. As they push forward to follow him I keep choking on the dust. This is wrong, it is all wrong."

There was no further information to be gained here, so I asked the client to move forward to the next significant moment in this life, but after a few times nothing happened so we returned to the "safe place", having closed the door firmly on that lifetime and given him several minutes to sit with these experiences and to reflect upon them I asked him what he made of all of that, and whether he still felt there were contracts made in past life that were still in effect.
"Why might your subconscious mind have shown these specific past lives? Was there anything to learn here?" I queried.
"I think, what I feel, what I understand now, is that I've always been this way. I've always felt the need to be strong and to be responsible. I don't think that was contractual, I think that is *me - I am at core responsible* and

it was that first life - seeing Jesus - where that impression was first made upon me, that I had to be different. My mission is my motivation, if you know what I mean. I got into advocacy work with a kind of missionary zeal. I suppose I have always wanted to make the world a better place, but I'm not going to carry the weight of that anymore. I'll do my bit to the best of my ability, but I'm not going to drive myself into the ground again."

"How did you reach that conclusion?"

I asked him.

"It was the little boy. When I was the little boy and I saw that terrible thing, I can hardly say it, I wanted to make it all stop, make it all better. I couldn't but I've been trying to make it stop, to make it better ever since in different lives," he said.

"Do we need to do more about those lives?"

"Yes, but I don't know how. I think they need to move on, they are stuck. I don't know how to help."

I asked Philip to call those parts of himself that had been prevented from developing in their past lives to come and join him. I asked him to have a conversation with them all, telling them what he learned from them, and I asked him to tell them all about his life now, perhaps to show them, in his mind, his life now, so that they might know something of their future. When this was done I asked Philip if he felt they needed to be integrated, but he said they already had the best parts of each self, past and present, integrated and that they needed to return to their rightful places. I asked him to call in a guide, or that most loving part of himself to direct them.

Philip said, "An angel has come, it is the Archangel Raphæl - I can't see him but have a sense of him, shifting facets of emerald-green. He has gathered them together and is taking them into the light."

"OK Philip, wait until that is done and then tell me what is happening." A few moments passed, then he said "It's all finished. They have all gone into the light; it feels really good. I feel lighter."

"And those contracts", I reminded him, "perhaps you can see those at your feet now, maybe as scrolls, or as papers held together, something like that."

"Yes, I can see them", he said, "but I don't feel like I can let them go."

I was just about to suggest some method of disposing of them when Philip interrupted me saying, "It's OK. The angel has come back. He took me by the wrist and made me release them into his hand. He tore the bundle through and is taking them away into the light too. He cancelled them himself for me. But it's up to me now. That's the sense I got."

WHO CHOOSES PLR?

In my experience, those who come to me for past life regression are from all walks of life. If I run through my mind all the people that have come to me for PLR so far there have been single working mums, a fireman, a police woman, a couple of nurses, a primary school teacher, a secondary school art teacher, a solicitor, an accountant, a GP, people aged 30-60 something, LGBT+ people, Hindus, Sikhs, a Buddhist, Christians, several Romanians, atheists and agnostics. Indeed, it would be quite difficult to say that "this type", or "that type", are *typical* of the clients for past life regression. I think that what they all have in common is that they were all seekers. They were curious people looking for insight, wisdom, perspective and knowledge about themselves – and that's great because a "let's see" outlook on life can take you to so many more places.

But there do seem to be themes that clients often bring up. We shall look at these in the next chapter.

WHY DO PEOPLE CHOOSE A PAST LIFE REGRESSION?

Farsickness

German has a word *fernweh* which can be translated as "farsickness". It is essentially an inexplicable desire to return to a place one has never visited, or a yearning for experiences never felt.

When I was a boy I was fascinated by the tales of King Arthur and the Knights of the Round Table. Therefore, I would immerse myself in any book or story that suggested a location of Camelot. I also loved the stories of Robin Hood. I desperately wanted to visit Sherwood Forest to see where Robin lived. The one place I did get to see was Stonehenge. It is even more awe-inspiring now than it was then. Now whilst I have been fascinated with these places, the heroes and legends, I have never felt that I might have had a past life in them. But many do.

Many seeking past life regression, and many who practice it, have experienced fascination *with a place* that isn't so much a desire to visit, but a *longing to return* be it a particular county in England, the River Thames, the Pyramids at Giza, the Coliseum in Rome, the Holy Land, or the Trail of Tears for example. There are even clients who come with a fascination for Lemuria, Atlantis or El Dorado and will have spent many years reading about these places. Very often they will be the only people they know among their friends and family who have such an interest.

HISTORICAL FIXATION

Many of us remember the first time we learned about the Vikings, the Romans or the Egyptians when we were in school, and for some of us what we learned then provided the germ of a lifelong love of, or fascination for the history and culture of particular peoples or nations, that grew with us. Indeed, fascination for a particular period is a common experience amongst those choosing past life regression.

Some people experience an almost palpable connection, or kinship with peoples and cultures they have never met. Often, I will hear how they felt so "at home" when visiting a previously unknown city, or country, and how easy it was for them to navigate, as if they had actually lived there, how their sense of longing for the place was great with a great surge of emotion upon arrival.

I would like to observe here, that in the majority of past life regressions I have conducted, the client has not recalled a lifetime in a place or period of history that has been to them a source of life-long passionate interest. It can be very disappointing for the client not to have an experience of being a Roman engineer, a Frankish knight, or a maid-in-waiting to Queen Victoria. So do bear this in mind. If you are a client your therapist cannot guarantee any outcome, if you are a therapist you need to make this clear to your client.

A problem without cause

Classic examples of this are the inability to find a suitable partner, erectile dysfunction after marriage, fear of drowning. When speaking to fellow practitioners of past life regression I have been told about the woman who came for a fear of drowning. Regression under hypnosis revealed a past life as a witch, in which the client had been tested with a ducking stool. Or the story of the client who seems to pick the worst men as partners. In regression she had experienced an unrivalled love for a man to whom she promised herself before he went off to battle, never to return. Or there is the man who had experienced erectile dysfunction only after marriage. Regression had revealed a previous marriage in which the couple were devout Christians who had believed in marriage for life, and promised to find one another in the afterlife. These last two are example of oaths and promises made in a previous life time that needed to be broken before the client could overcome their problem in their life.

RECURRING DREAMS

The recurring dream is for many of us an unremarkable experience. It isn't unknown for children to have the same dream over and over again, or for an adult to experience recurring dreams, for example in times of stress around exams, or pregnancy. But some people will have the same or similar dreams over and over again throughout their lives, about a particular place, period in history, or even a family or group of people. It is entirely natural that those experiencing those dreams will want to discover more about them, to discover if those dreams have an origin in a past life.

FAMILY TREE RESEARCH

I have seen a number of clients who have been very interested in genealogy. Some have been very successful in tracing back their families and collating an impressive collection of evidence, whilst others struggle a bit. So far, I have never regressed a person who was their own great grandfather in a previous life, but I suspect that there are many therapists in the world who have. I suppose it is the lure of knowing more about where one comes from, or about the lives of people like those in one's family tree that eventually leads some clients to our doors. I do wonder at times whether the deep interest in family history isn't actually at some level a replacement for knowing one's own previous lifetimes in the absence of knowledge about past life regression.

ALIEN ABDUCTION

This isn't really within the scope of this book, but I and a number of my colleagues have been approached at various times by people who are either certain that they were abducted by aliens, or suspect they might have been abducted by aliens and wish to be regressed to that time in this lifetime to remember what happened to them. I suspect the reason we are approached is because we are seen as being more open minded; and I certainly hope that we are, because it isn't our place to judge but to assist. Then of course there are those clients whose regressions divulge previous lives as aliens, gods and other off-worlders.

CHOOSING A THERAPIST

It is advisable to take some time in finding the right hypnotherapist for you. There are, after all, thousands to choose from, therefore creating a short list can be daunting. Generally, a referral from someone you know and trust is a good place to start looking for a therapist. However, if you don't know anyone who has visited a hypnotherapist who specialises in past life regression, where do you start? If going to someone as near to you as possible is most important to you, you can whittle down the list of potential therapists with a simple Google search for "past life regression near me." That is certain to bring up for you a number of paid advertisements and those whose offices are nearby.
There are a few things that you might want to consider.

The therapist's training

You might want to ask about the hypnotherapist's training. New hypnotherapists are often very good because they are up to date with current thinking and haven't had time to forget, but neither have they had time to develop their skills, and there are very few training schools that specialise in past life regression. Therefore, you might want to ask some direct questions about experience. Most therapists will be very happy to tell you about their training and experience and the areas that they have an interest in.

ASK ABOUT INSURANCE

You can also ask a therapist you are interested in working with whether they are insured. Most professional and ethical hypnotherapists are insured. They choose to be for the sake of your confidence in them and because it is usually a requirement of their professional association.

However, if you haven't the time for all those questions, then you can always go straight to a directory of professional hypnotherapists. It just so happens that there is an international directory of professional hypnotherapists known as The Past Life Therapists Association – the PLTA. When a hypnotherapist applies to become a member of the PLTA they have to submit their proof of training and current insurance cover.

The directory of the PLTA website contains a lot of information about the various therapists listed so that you can easily choose someone.

The Past Life Therapists Association is a UK based international accrediting body for past life regression and therapy, life between life therapy – which is sometime called interlife therapy, and future life progression. It was established to recognise, support and promote therapists working in these areas. In fact, the PLTA tends to regard these as specialised, or stand-alone therapies in their own right with an understanding of the more spiritual aspects of therapy. Therefore, you will find that the members are very open to a wide variety of philosophies and outlooks on life.

You can find the directory here – www.pastliferegression.co.uk.

WHEN HYPNOSIS ISN'T RECOMMENDED

Regression work of any kind can uncover strong and unpleasant memories and emotions. We must then be careful how we proceed as therapists, and prospective clients are often well advised to let sleeping dogs lie.

Sadly, for some people hypnosis isn't possible. This will usually be because of a medical condition and/or medication that makes this kind of therapy unreliable.

SERIOUS MENTAL HEALTH CONDITIONS

Unless a therapist is specially trained to work with people who have schizophrenia, bi-polar disorder, or emotional unstable personality disorder, for example, they will generally not work with people who suffer serious mental health challenges. This is because we cannot predict how a person will respond, and because it is felt among some experts that there is a possibility of exacerbating the symptoms of a person with such a mental health challenge that it best to leave well alone.

PREGNANCY

Most hypnotherapists I know will not work with a person in their first trimester of pregnancy. There are some very special circumstances when this guidance would be over-ruled, but since a past life regression is unlikely to be necessary during pregnancy it would be my advice to wait till you have delivered your baby before pursing PLR.

There are multiple reasons why hypnosis during pregnancy is not always advisable. If you are a therapist and are not sure of the reasons, consult with your supervisor. If you are a potential client you might like to consult your primary medical caregiver in the first instance, and seek the opinion of a therapist you trust.

Seizures

Where there is a risk that deep relaxation or strong emotion may lead to a seizure, past life regression would be contra-indicated. We always want to work with the safety of the client in mind. Sometimes that means disappointing people. But the well-being of the client is paramount.

HEALING CRISES

A healing crisis can most easily be described as a temporary worsening of symptoms arising from therapeutic action. A damaged limb or muscle might feel worse after physiotherapy, whilst certain diets or detox regimes can bring on flu-like symptoms.

During talking therapy of various kinds, it is very common indeed for clients to feel somewhat worse for a few days as memories, associations, and feelings are stirred up. Therapy can be a bit like stirring the bottom of a pond at times; all kinds of muck can be released into what were relatively clear waters.

We have all had the experience at some time or another of being tired and having aching muscles after some exertion that whilst causing fatigue also did us good. We are also familiar with experiences of the past that were uncomfortable being beneficial later. After a session of therapy, a person can feel different, and sometimes they can feel worse. Sometimes therapy will elicit feelings the client hasn't experienced before, or for a very long time.

It can be unsettling to have the experience of being a murderer in a past life, and therefore a course of past life regression therapy can sometimes be required. Some of Dr Brian Weiss' patients underwent a series of regressions over a number of months bringing relief to a wide variety of symptoms. You can read about these in his books.

Most of the time past life regression is very gentle, and distressing experiences are settled towards the end of the session, or afterwards in conversation with the therapist. But sometimes the shake-up we received stays with us for a bit, challenging us to re-evaluate aspects of our lives, such as our careers, or relationships. This isn't always something we want to do, but often it is something we *need* to do. Therefore, it is advisable for therapists to talk to their clients about the possible effects of past life regression, and for clients to ask about the potential need for further assistance.

By the way, further assistance doesn't necessarily mean further hypnotherapy. Past life regression can bring you to a point where your mental and emotional obstacles from a past life or current life are resolved, but the expertise of another are required to take you further.

For example, let's suppose you sank with the Bismarck in a previous life and now have a fear of water. Your past life regression therapist can help remove your phobia, but they usually won't be able to teach you to swim or water-ski. Or if your inability to make money in this life, was due to a vow of poverty made in a previous life, your hypnotherapist can help you revoke that old vow, but you might need the services of a business coach before you start to make a financial success of your business.

PAST LIFE READING

In cases where a past life regression is not advisable then some might find that a past life reading is an acceptable alternative. The way this works is that a person, occasionally trained as a therapist, but who is also a medium or psychic will tune into the person and 'read' their past lives for them. These can also elicit strong feelings, but are often gentler that a past life regression in which the client might relive the trauma of a past life. They can be just as healing, and provide a great deal of insight for the person receiving the reading – the sitter.

SURROGATE REGRESSION

Another alternative is that the person seeking regression but who cannot undergo hypnosis – perhaps they simply haven't the time – can arrange for a past life regression practitioner to work with a medium who will act as a surrogate for the client. That is to say the psychic, tuning into the client, undergoes regression whilst a recording is made. The transcription of the recording, or perhaps the recording itself, is then sent to the client with the data obtained assumed to be representative of the client's past lives.

TRAINING IN PAST LIFE REGRESSION

Past life regression and therapy is a very interesting field of study and professional practice. Assuming you are already trained as a practitioner of hypnotherapy you can find many courses that will add past life regression to your core skills. Some online training providers will certify you with a few hours of training, others will give you a great deal more material to work with and insist upon your passing a qualifying exam.

The Past Life Therapists Association provides trusted, tried and tested training by correspondence to qualified hypnotherapists with a

- Diploma in Past Life Regression and Hypnotherapy
- Advanced Diploma in Past Life Regression and Therapy
- Future Life Progression
- Past Life Energy Therapy (a favourite among those who are Reiki trained)
- Interlife or Life Between Life Therapy

There is also a listing of accredited trainers who offer live training. You can find more here https://pastliferegression.co.uk/training/

If you are a therapist and would like to join The Past Life

Therapists Association you can do that here: www.pastliferegression.co.uk .

OTHER BOOKS BY GAVIN BOWTELL

If have enjoyed this book you might want to read ***Tapping for Emotional Freedom – An EFT Pocket Book***.

It is a brilliant resource for anyone interested in self-improvement, or who needs a self-help guide that is clear and easy to follow.

Tapping into Emotional Freedom is a concise introduction to the transformative power of Emotional Freedom Technique (EFT), also known as tapping.

EFT combines the benefits of ancient acupressure with modern psychotherapy streamlined to a handy process for resolving the stresses and anxieties of modern living, and more serious matters too.

This book puts the power of therapy into your hands. EFT is gentle, fast, versatile and easy to learn.

The book contains illustrations of all the EFT tapping points for the Full Recipe so that you will learn exactly where to tap quickly and without difficulty.

Suitable for all readers from 18 upwards. This book can be used at home or taken anyway to college, to work, or on holiday.
Wherever you are, you can benefit from the power of EFT.

WHAT IS EFT?

EFT/Tapping can be thought of as "emotional acupuncture", except there are no needles involved. Instead you tap specific points on the head and body that are related to your body's energy meridians.
EFT can be used alongside conventional medical treatment, counselling and coaching systems.

EFT or Emotional Freedom Technique is a tool used by thousands of psychologists, therapists and coaches across the globe, to help free their clients from limiting beliefs, negative thoughts, traumatic memories and painful emotions.

WHAT CAN IT BE USED FOR?

EFT may be used to help with:
Stress
Anxiety
Depression
Fears
Pain
Phobias
Cravings
PTSD
Weight loss
Sports performance
Highly sensitive personalities
Confidence
Self-esteem and more.

HOW CAN EFT HELP YOU?

EFT can help you to change limiting beliefs and realise your potential. It can help you melt away stress, rob anxiety of its power and draw the sting of painful memories.

WHAT YOU WILL LEARN FROM THIS BOOK?

You will learn the EFT tapping points.
How to create a set-up phrase and affirmation.
How to create a reminder phrase, and why this is important.
You will learn the exact location of the tapping points and the order in which to tap.
You will learn how to chart your progress.
How to change the 'writing on your walls'.
How to utilise the Personal Peace Procedure.
And 10 Great Ideas for optimising your personal EFT practice.

WHAT IS INCLUDED?

Illustrations designed specifically for this book.

Links to academic articles.

Links to video demonstrations that you can tap along to.

Details of how to obtain EFT training.

A book written by a practitioner with 10+ years' experience of using EFT.

SUPERVISION, TRAINING AND CONTINUING PROFESSIONAL DEVELOPMENT.

Supervision

Gavin Bowtell is registered as a clinical supervisor and is available for one-to-one differential and peer supervision.

Details can be found through the Essex Mind Coach website: www.essexmindcoach.co.uk .

Continuing Professional Development

In addition to supervising six past life regression and therapy correspondence courses he also offers training in the EFT:
Foundation Certificate Course, and the
Advanced Practitioner Qualification.

Also available is the course:
Affirmative Therapy – Working Successfully with LGBTQIA+ Clients written by Steven Harold and Gavin Bowtell.

You can find these here https://essexmindcoach.co.uk/training/

SPECIALIST SCRIPTS FOR PROFESSIONAL HYPNOTHERAPISTS.

Also available through the website are specialist hypnotherapy scripts for the professional hypnotherapist.
For example:

- For Mothers:
  accepting your gay son
- For Fathers:
  accepting your gay son
- Phantom Limb Syndrome recovery
- Bisexuality: self-acceptance
- Non-binary: self-acceptance
- Health anxiety
- Depersonalisation recovery

and more besides

You can find these here www.essexmindcoach.co.uk/therapist-resources/

Audio downloads
A small selection of audio downloads is also available for rest, relaxation, resilience and past life regression here:

https://essexmindcoach.co.uk/audio-downloads/

These recordings are not a replacement for conventional medical treatment, they should not be used by people with serious mental health issues, and certainly should never be used whilst operating machinery or driving, or at any time when your full attention is required as they ask you to close your eyes.

MEET THE AUTHOR

I'm Gavin Bowtell. I am a therapist living and working in Chigwell, Essex. Before becoming a hypnotherapist I worked in customer services, luxury retail and rail transport operations.
At the time of writing I am the new Chair of the Past Life Therapists Association, following the retirement of its founder Andrew Hillsdon, FPLTA – a much respected teacher and colleague.
I am a guest speaker at the Kent Institute of Clinical Hypnotherapy where I deliver workshops on EFT, and have also provided CPD for the Association of Professional Hypnosis and Psychotherapy.

I live with my partner and our five cats. I enjoy the outdoors, gardening, reading, and playing the guitar and ukulele – Nora and Rob are to blame for the noise I make.

Special thanks go to David Chapman and to Mark Vince for proofreading the book.

Printed in Great Britain
by Amazon

190fa794-05c6-4547-8c12-4ed8c6494632R02